Macmillan/McGraw-Hill **TIMELINKS**

People and Places

PROGRAM AUTHORS

James A. Banks
Kevin P. Colleary
Linda Greenow
Walter C. Parker
Emily M. Schell
Dinah Zike

CONTRIBUTORS

Raymond C. Jones
Irma M. Olmedo

Macmillan/McGraw-Hill

Geography

PROGRAM AUTHORS

James A. Banks, Ph.D.
Kerry and Linda Killinger Professor
of Diversity Studies and Director, Center
for Multicultural Education
University of Washington
Seattle, Washington

Kevin P. Colleary, Ed.D.
Curriculum and Teaching Department
Graduate School of Education
Fordham University
New York, New York

Linda Greenow, Ph.D.
Associate Professor and Chair
Department of Geography
State University of New York at New Paltz
New Paltz, New York

Walter C. Parker, Ph.D.
Professor of Social Studies Education,
Adjunct Professor of Political Science
University of Washington
Seattle, Washington

Emily M. Schell, Ed.D.
Visiting Professor, Teacher Education
San Diego State University
San Diego, California

Dinah Zike
Educational Consultant
Dinah-Mite Activities, Inc.
San Antonio, Texas

CONTRIBUTORS

Raymond C. Jones, Ph.D.
Director of Secondary Social Studies
Education
Wake Forest University
Winston-Salem, North Carolina

Irma M. Olmedo
Associate Professor
University of Illinois-Chicago
College of Education
Chicago, Illinois

HISTORIANS/SCHOLARS

Brooks Green, Ph.D.
Associate Professor of Geography
University of Central Arkansas
Conway, Arkansas

GRADE LEVEL REVIEWERS

Kathleen Clark
Second Grade Teacher
Edison Elementary
Fraser, Michigan

Patricia Hinchliff
Second Grade Teacher
West Woods School
Hamden, Connecticut

Pamela South
Second Grade Teacher
Greenwood Elementary School
Princess Anne, Maryland

Karen Starr
Second Grade Teacher
Arthur Froberg Elementary School
Rockford, Illinois

EDITORIAL ADVISORY BOARD

Bradley R. Bakle
Assistant Superintendent
East Allen County Schools
New Haven, Indiana

Marilyn Barr
Assistant Superintendent for Instruction
Clyde-Savannah Central School
Clyde, New York

Lisa Bogle
Elementary Coordinator, K-5
Rutherford County Schools
Murfreesboro, Tennessee

Janice Buselt
Campus Support, Primary and ESOL
Wichita Public Schools
Wichita, Kansas

Kathy Cassioppi
Social Studies Coordinator
Rockford Public Schools, District 205
Rockford, Illinois

Denise Johnson, Ph.D.
Social Studies Supervisor
Knox County Schools
Knoxville, Tennessee

Steven Klein, Ph.D.
Social Studies Coordinator
Illinois School District U-46
Elgin, Illinois

Sondra Markman
Curriculum Director
Warren Township Board of Education
Warren Township, New Jersey

Cathy Nelson
Social Studies Coordinator
Columbus Public Schools
Columbus, Ohio

Holly Pies
Social Studies Coordinator
Vigo County Schools
Terre Haute, Indiana

Avon Ruffin
Social Studies County Supervisor
Winston-Salem/Forsyth Schools
Lewisville, North Carolina

Chuck Schierloh
Social Studies Curriculum Team Leader
Lima City Schools
Lima, Ohio

Bob Shamy
Social Studies Supervisor
East Brunswick Public Schools
East Brunswick, New Jersey

Judy Trujillo
Social Studies Coordinator
Columbia Missouri School District
Columbia, Missouri

Gayle Voyles
Director of the Center for Economic
Education
Kansas City School District
Kansas City, Missouri

Todd Wigginton
Coordinator of Social Studies K-12
Metropolitan Nashville Public Schools
Nashville, Tennessee

Students with print disabilities may be eligible to obtain an accessible, audio version of the pupil edition of this textbook. Please call Recording for the Blind & Dyslexic at 1-800-221-4792 for complete information.

learning through listening

The McGraw-Hill Companies

Macmillan McGraw-Hill

People and Places
Table of Contents

Skills and Features

Maps

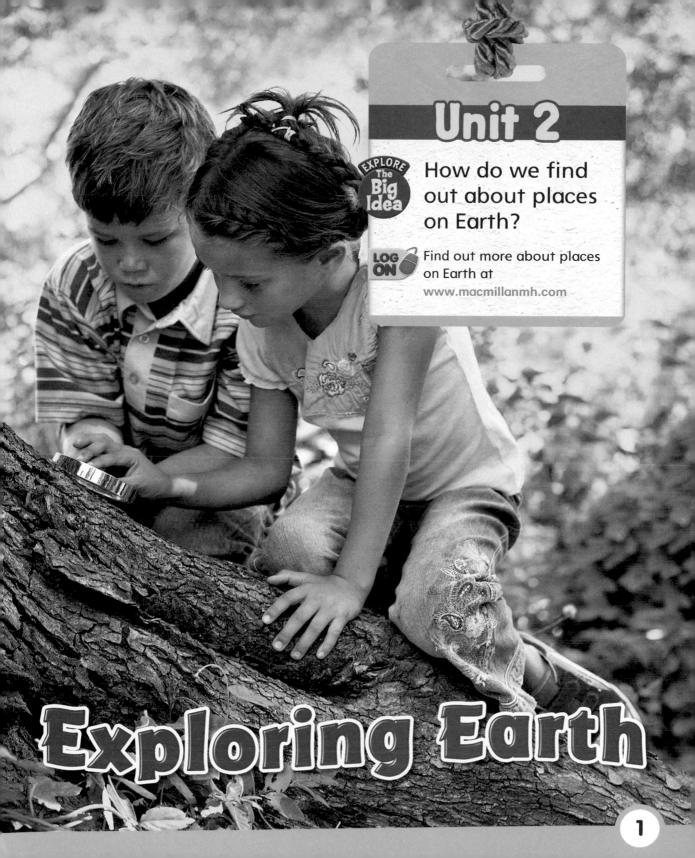

EXPLORE The Big Idea

How do we find out about places on Earth?

LOG ON

Find out more about places on Earth at
www.macmillanmh.com

Exploring Earth

People, Places, and Events

Neighbors

Neighbors in New Orleans have fun together.

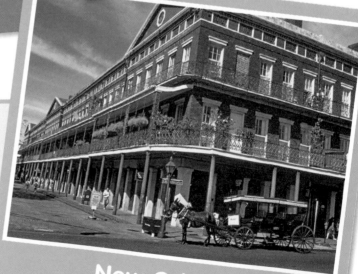

New Orleans

New Orleans is an urban community in the state of Louisiana.

Hurricane Katrina

Neighbors in New Orleans helped each other during a big storm called **Hurricane Katrina**.

All About Location

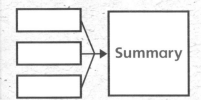

A Place for Everything

A **location** is the place where something is. Your house is in a location. Your bed is in a location. A location can be large or small.

Jordan made a map of his bedroom. A map makes it easy to see the locations of things.

 Which square tells the location of Jordan's bed?

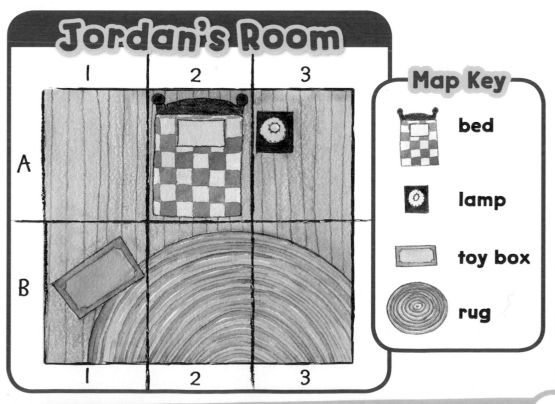

Talking About Locations

There are ways to tell locations. Absolute location tells the exact spot where something is. Your home address tells the absolute location of your home.

The absolute location of the blue house is 12 Elm Street. What are the absolute locations of the red and yellow houses?

Relative location tells where something is by comparing it to another thing. Words like *above*, *next to*, and *below* tell the relative location of something.

 What is the relative location of the yellow house?

Check Understanding

1. **Vocabulary** What is one way to tell the **location** of your desk?

2. **Summarize** What are absolute and relative location?

3. 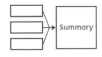 How are addresses helpful?

Vocabulary

state

country

border

continent

flow chart

Reading Skill

Summarize

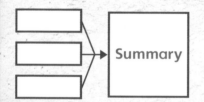

Summary

Where We Live

Cleveland

Ohio

★ Columbus

Cincinnati

We Live in a Country

Meet Lana. Lana lives in the urban community of Cleveland. Cleveland is located in the **state** of Ohio.

A state is part of the United States of America. The United States of America is the name of our **country**. A country is the land and the people who live there.

 Can you find your state on the map?

We Live on a Continent

Some countries have neighbors. Mexico is our neighbor to the south. Our neighbor to the north is Canada.

We share **borders** with these two countries. A border is a line on a map that separates one state or country from another.

United States

Together, the United States, its neighbors, and other countries form one large area of land called a **continent**. Lana lives on the continent of North America. You do, too!

 What countries are neighbors of the United States?

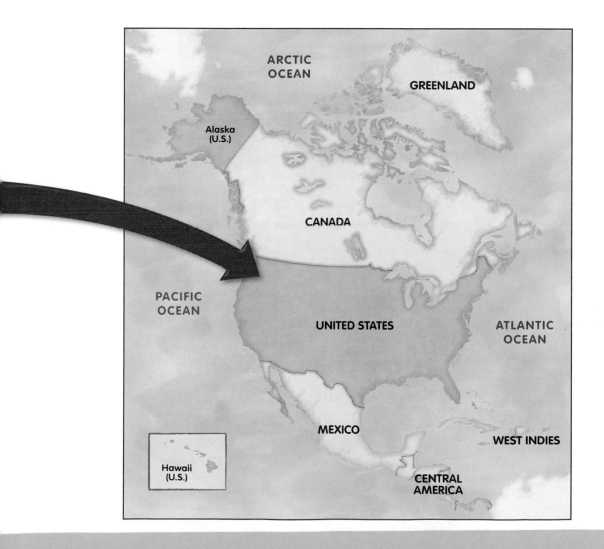

North America is one of Earth's seven continents.

NORTH AMERICA
UNITED STATES

ATLANTIC OCEAN

Equator

PACIFIC OCEAN

SOUTH AMERICA

Our World

Look at the map of the world. Earth's continents are Africa, Antarctica, Asia, Australia, Europe, North America, and South America. These seven continents make up the land on Earth.

 Does Earth have more land or water?

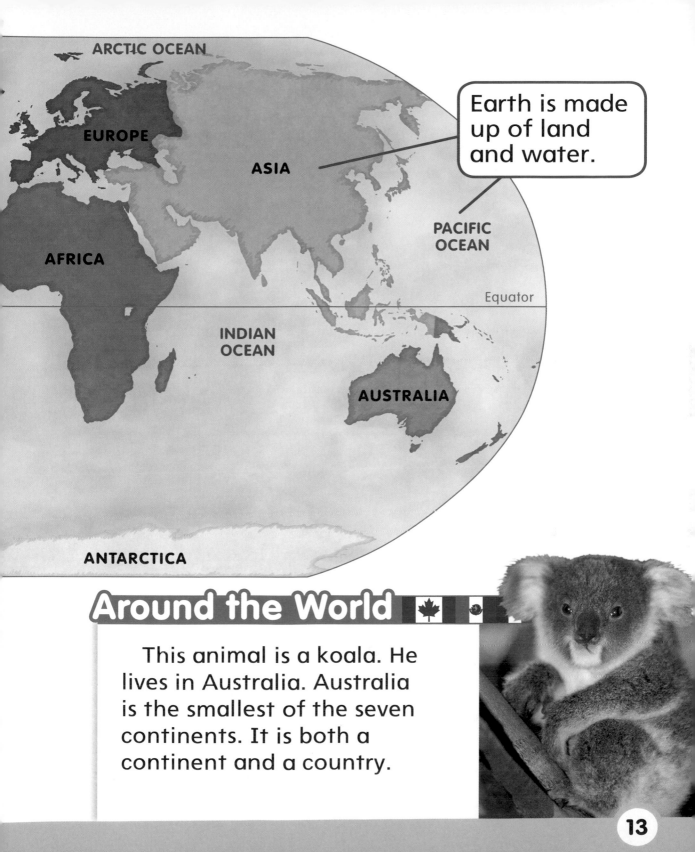

ARCTIC OCEAN

EUROPE

ASIA

AFRICA

PACIFIC OCEAN

Earth is made up of land and water.

Equator

INDIAN OCEAN

AUSTRALIA

ANTARCTICA

Around the World

This animal is a koala. He lives in Australia. Australia is the smallest of the seven continents. It is both a continent and a country.

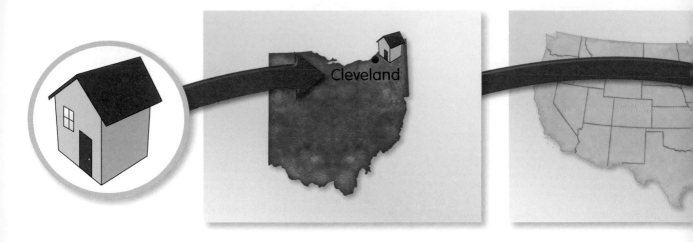

Cleveland

Our Location in the World

This **flow chart** shows where Lana lives. A flow chart uses arrows to show information in an order.

Find Lana's house. Now find Lana's house in Cleveland, Ohio. Follow the arrows to bigger and bigger locations.

 Name each place Lana lives in order.

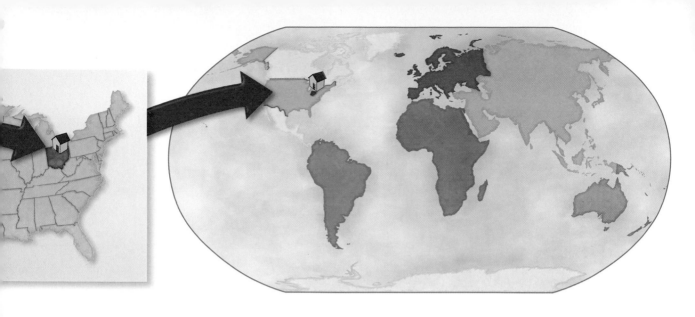

Check Understanding

1. **Vocabulary** What **states** share a **border** with your **state**?

2. **Summarize** Tell where you live using bigger and bigger locations.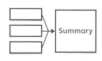

3. **EXPLORE The Big Idea** What can you use to find the location of your state?

Land and Water

Vocabulary

desert

landform

valley   river

plain   lake

island   hill

peninsula

Reading Skill

Summarize

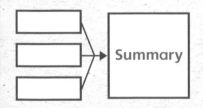

Summary

Across Our Country

Sally and her family live in Phoenix, Arizona. Phoenix is a city in the Sonoran **Desert**. A desert is a dry area with very little rain.

Sally took a trip to see her grandparents in Rumson, New Jersey. She took pictures of water and **landforms**. A landform is a shape of land on Earth.

 What is a desert?

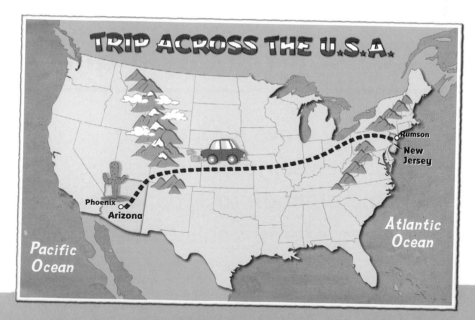

TRIP ACROSS THE U.S.A.

Rumson
New Jersey
Phoenix
Arizona
Atlantic Ocean
Pacific Ocean

flowers in a valley

Through the Mountains

Sally's family drove through the Rocky Mountains. Mountains are the highest kind of landform. The low area between mountains is called a **valley**.

They drove on a bridge that crossed over the Mississippi **River**. A river is a single stream of water that flows into a larger body of water, like an ocean.

The Mississippi River is the second longest river in the United States. It flows all the way from Minnesota to Louisiana.

 What is a valley?

Mississippi River

On the Plain

In Indiana, Sally saw a lot of flat land. Flat land is called a **plain**. A plain is good land for farming. Sally saw farms with wheat and corn growing on plains.

This cow lives on a plain. Moo!

Ballast Island

In Ohio, Sally's family stopped at **Lake** Erie for a picnic. A lake is a body of water that has land all around it. It is smaller than an ocean. Sally took a picture of an **island** in the lake. An island is a landform that has water all around it.

 What is a lake?

Places
Lake Itasca

Lake Itasca is in Minnesota. It is at the beginning of the Mississippi River.

To the Ocean

Sally's family drove through **hills** in Pennsylvania. A hill is higher than the land around it but not as high as a mountain.

A **peninsula** is a landform with water on all sides except one. Sally knew she would see her grandparents soon after they drove past Sandy Hook peninsula in New Jersey. She could not wait to show them the photos of her trip!

What is a peninsula?

hills

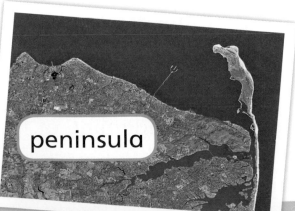

peninsula

Grandma and Grandpa live
in Rumson, New Jersey.

Check Understanding

1. **Vocabulary** What two **landforms** are higher than the land around them?

2. **Summarize** How are the plains used?

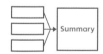

3. **EXPLORE The Big Idea** What did the pictures in this lesson show?

Use Landform Maps

Vocabulary

landform map

A **landform map** uses colors to show the different kinds of water and land. Use the map and map key to answer the questions.

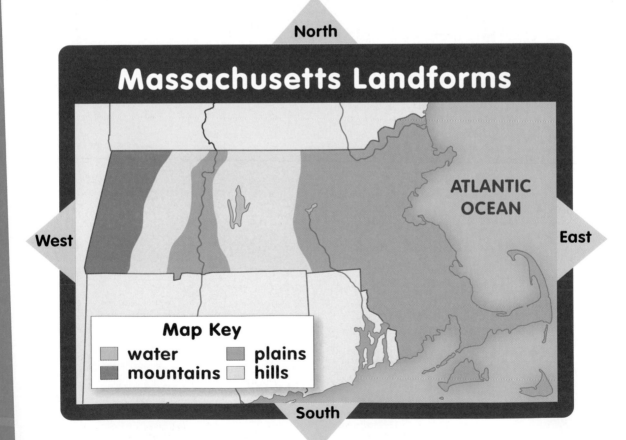

North

Massachusetts Landforms

West

ATLANTIC OCEAN

East

South

Map Key
- water
- mountains
- plains
- hills

■ water

■ mountains

■ plains

■ hills

Try the Skill

1. What does a **landform map** show?

2. Are there more hills or mountains in Massachusetts?

Writing Activity
Make a landform map of your state. Write about your favorite landform.

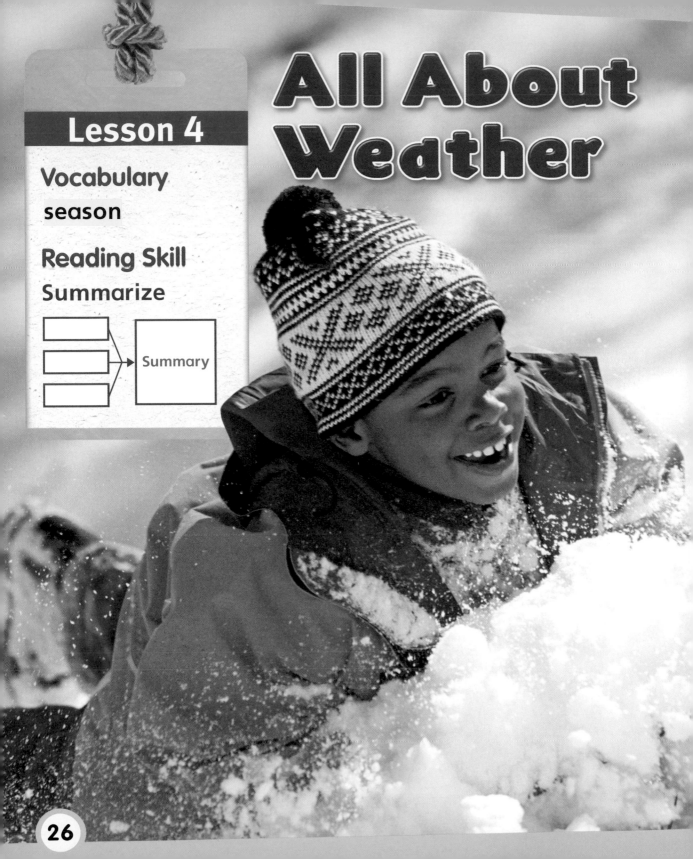

All About Weather

Lesson 4

Vocabulary
season

Reading Skill
Summarize

Summary

Weather Here and There

It is February. "It is snowy and cold here!" Cole says. He lives in Wisconsin.

In Alabama, Jada says, "It is sunny and warm here today." On the same day, weather in different places can be very different.

What is the weather like today where you live?

Weather Changes

Weather can change from day to day. One day it is sunny, and the next day it is rainy. When we talk about rain or snow or how hot or cold it is, we are talking about the weather.

Sunny day

Rainy day

Flowers bloom in the spring.

Summer can be hot and sunny.

Leaves turn colors in the fall.

Winter can be cold and snowy.

Weather can change from **season** to season, too. A season is a time of year. Spring, summer, fall, and winter are the four seasons. In many places, weather is colder in the winter and warmer in the summer.

 How do you enjoy the four seasons?

29

Thunderstorms have lightning and heavy rain.

Storms

Sometimes we have storms. Rainstorms, snowstorms, and thunderstorms are three kinds of storms.

A big snowstorm is called a blizzard. A very strong wind and rainstorm that moves across the ocean is called a hurricane.

Event
Tornado

A tornado is a storm with very strong winds that blow around in a circle. In 2006 a tornado struck in Indiana.

When a hurricane reaches land, it can cause problems as Hurricane Katrina did in 2005.

Hurricane Katrina

 What are two kinds of storms?

Check Understanding

1. **Vocabulary** What are the four **seasons**?

2. **Summarize** What are ways the weather can change?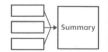

3.  What is a hurricane?

Earth's Resources

Vocabulary

natural resource

Reading Skill

Summarize

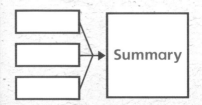

Natural Resources

A **natural resource** is something in nature that people use. Water is a natural resource we can use again and again. We use water to drink and to grow and cook food.

Rocks, trees, and soil are also natural resources. We can use rocks to build things like dams and bridges. We use the wood from trees to build our homes. Trees need soil to grow.

How do we use trees?

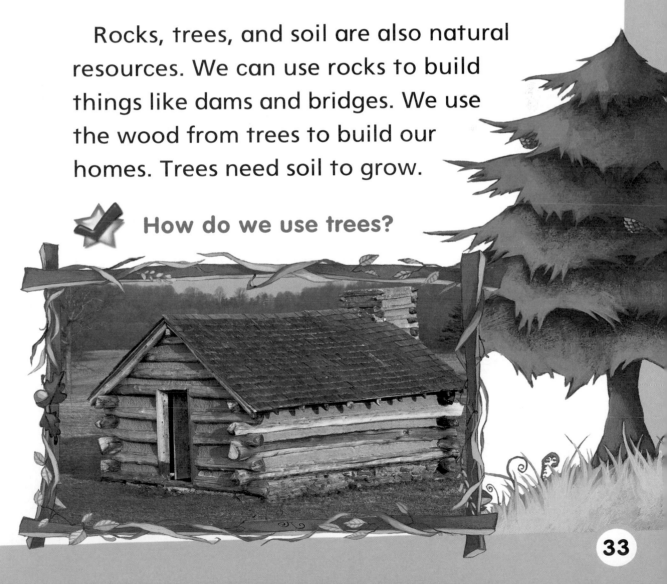

Kinds of Natural Resources

Some natural resources can run out. We use coal or oil to heat our homes. If we run out of coal and oil, they will be gone.

We can save natural resources, like coal and oil, by using less. Energy from the sun heats this home.

Some natural resources, like trees, can be replaced. When we use a tree, we can plant another one to take its place.

 How can we replace a tree?

Check Understanding

1. **Vocabulary** What is a **natural resource**?

2. **Summarize** How is water used?

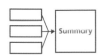

3. What are two natural resources we could run out of forever?

Citizenship

Democracy in Action

Respecting Nature

We respect nature when we care about our natural resources and all living things. Respect means to treat as important. Read what happened when Marie showed Anne the bird eggs.

Anne helped Marie to respect nature. What would you do?

Oh, look at the bird eggs, Anne! They are so cute. Let us take them home.

No, we should not do that Marie. The baby birds cannot hatch if we take the eggs away.

Oh, you are right. We must not touch them.

Lesson 6

We Change Earth

Vocabulary

crops

reduce

reuse

recycle

Reading Skill

Summarize

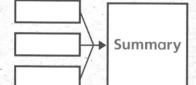

Summary

We Build and Dig

Build it big! Dig it deep! How do we change Earth? We build dams across rivers to hold water. We build roads and bridges and dig tunnels to connect our communities.

 What changes have people made to Earth in your community?

Farmers use machines to clear the land.

Earth Is Our Home

Farmers change Earth, too. They clear the land to plant **crops**. Crops are plants we grow to use for food and other things.

What happens when we build roads and cities and clear the land? Some plants and animals lose their homes. Some land must be saved as homes for plants and animals.

What happens when we put trash in our lakes and rivers? The water can become polluted. Polluted means dirty. We need clean water to use today and in the future.

 Why is it important to take care of Earth?

People
Rachel Carson

People learned about a poison called DDT because of a scientist named Rachel Carson. She said, "Now I can believe I have at least helped a little."

Reduce, Reuse, Recycle

There are many ways to take care of Earth. We can **reduce** our use of natural resources. Reduce means to use less. Eddie turns the water off while brushing his teeth.

We can **reuse** things we already have. Reuse means to use again. This boat was made with empty milk cartons.

We can **recycle** glass, plastic, paper, and metal. Recycle means change into something new.

 What could you reuse?

Check Understanding

1. **Vocabulary** What are some things that you can **recycle**?

2. **Summarize** How do people change Earth?

3. 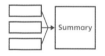 How can we take care of Earth?

Review and Assess

Vocabulary

Choose the vocabulary word that best completes each sentence.

country   **island**   **crops**

1. _____ are plants we grow to use or eat.

2. The United States is a _____ on the continent of North America.

3. An _____ is land that has water all around it.

Critical Thinking

4. What are ways you can reduce your use of some natural resources?

5. Why is it hard to grow crops in the desert?

Use Landform Maps

Use the landform map of Pennsylvania to answer the question.

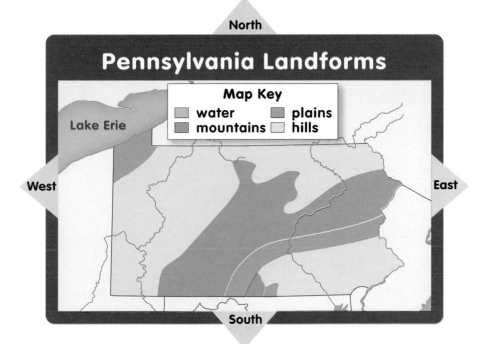

North

Pennsylvania Landforms

Map Key
- water
- mountains
- plains
- hills

Lake Erie

West

East

South

6. What do you see most of in Pennsylvania?

A. mountains

B. water

C. plains

D. hills

The Big Idea

Geography Activity

Make a Poster

1 Find out about a place near your community.

2 Draw a picture of the place on a poster.

3 Write sentences under your picture that tell about the place.

4 Show your poster to the class. Tell them how you learned about the place.

Lake Michigan

Lake Michigan is one of the Great Lakes. It has places for camping and boating.

Picture Glossary

B

border A line on a map that separates one state or country from another. *Can you see the* **border** *that separates Canada from the United States?* (page 10)

C

continent One of the seven largest pieces of land on Earth. *We live on the* **continent** *of North America.* (page 11)

country The land and the people who live there. *The name of our* **country** *is the United States of America.* (page 9)

crops Plants we grow to use or eat. *The farmer will grow* **crops** *of watermelon to sell.* (page 40)

D

desert A dry area of land. *We saw cacti plants when we took our trip through the* **desert**. (page 17)

F

flow chart A chart that uses arrows to show information in an order. *This* **flow chart** *shows bigger and bigger locations.* (page 14)

H

hill Land that is higher than the land around it but not as high as a mountain. *We walked up these beautiful hills together.* (page 22)

I

island A landform that has water all around it. *We sailed our boat to Ballast Island in Lake Erie.* (page 21)

L

lake A body of water with land all around it. *We went fishing in Lake Itasca.* (page 21)

landform A shape of land on Earth. *A mountain is the highest kind of landform.* (page 17)

landform map A map that uses colors to show different kinds of water and land. *This landform map shows water, mountains, plains, and hills in Massachusetts.* (page 24)

location The place where something is. *The location of the teddy bear is on the bed.* (page 5)

N

natural resource Something in nature that people use. *Water is a natural resource.* (page 33)

P

peninsula A landform that has water on all sides except one. *Sandy Hook is a peninsula in New Jersey.* (page 22)

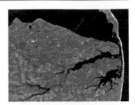

plain A flat area of land. *A plain is a good location for growing wheat.* (page 20)

R

recycle To change a thing into something new and useful. *Old newspapers can be recycled into new ones.* (page 43)

reduce To use less of something. *Eddie reduces water by turning off the faucet while brushing his teeth.* (page 42)

reuse To use something again. *Mr. Smith helped us reuse milk cartons to make our boat.* (page 42)

river A stream of water that often flows into a larger body of water. *We took a boat ride on the Mississippi **River**.* (page 19)

season One of the four times of the year. *Fall is the **season** when leaves turn red, yellow, and brown.* (page 29)

state One part of a country. *The **state** of Ohio is one part of the United States.* (page 9)

V

valley The low area between mountains. *We walked down the mountain to find the **valley**.* (page 18)

Index

This index lists many things you can find in your book. It tells the page numbers on which they are found. If you see the letter *m* before a page number, you will find a map on that page.

Index

Credits

Maps: XNR

Illustrations:
4-5: Kathleen Kemly. 6: Laurence Cleyet-Merle. 7: Laurence Cleyet-Merle. 18-19: Terry Kovalcik. 20-21: Terry Kovalcik. 22-23: Terry Kovalcik. 27: Bridget Starr Taylor. 33: Laurence Cleyet-Merle. 34: Kristin Varner. 35: Laurence Cleyet-Merle. 40: Laurence Cleyet-Merle. 39: Micreau Catunsanu.

Photography Credits: All Photographs are by Macmillan/McGraw-hill (MMH) except as noted below.

1: Devan/zefa/CORBIS. 2: (br) Scott Berner/Index Stock Imagery; (cl) Bob Sacha/CORBIS; (cr) Sherwood Hoffman/Index Stock Imagery. 3: (br) C Squared Studios/Getty Images; (tc) Jason Reed/Reuters/CORBIS. 8: (fg) Ken Karp for MMH; Andre Jenny/Alamy Images. 10: Ken Karp for MMH. 13: (br) Gary Bell/zefa/CORBIS. 15: (c) Andre Jenny/Alamy Images. 16: George H. H. Huey Photography. 17: (tr) Stockbyte/PunchStock. 18: (c) James Randklev/Getty Images. 19: (bc) Charles McDowell/Grant Heilman Photography. 20: (br) CORBIS; (c) Darrell Gulin/CORBIS. 21: (br) Dominique Braud/Animals Animals; (tc) John and Carol Rees. 22: (bl) Tom Till/Tom Till Photography; (br) AirPhoto USA/TerraServer.com. 23: (c) James Randklev/Getty Images; (tl) BlueMoon Stock/PunchStock. 25: (cl) Jerry and Marcy Monkman/EcoPhotography.com/Alamy Images; (cr) Ed Langan/Index Stock Imagery; (tl) J. David Andrews/Masterfile; (tr) LMR Group/Alamy Images. 26:

Ariel Skelley/CORBIS. 27: (bc) image100/PunchStock. 28: (bl) Glyn Jones/CORBIS. 29: (cl) Gary Buss/Getty Images; (cr) Getty Images; (tl) Gary Buss/Getty Images; (tr) Gary Buss/Getty Images. 30: (br) Peter Arnold, Inc./Alamy Images; (t) Larry Lee Photography/CORBIS. 31: (c) Gary Buss/Getty Images; (tr) Mike Theiss/Jim Reed Photography/CORBIS. 32: Garry Black/Masterfile. 33: (bl) Joseph Sohm; ChromoSohm Inc/CORBIS. 34: (br) Chinch Gryniewicz/CORBIS; (tl) Reuters/CORBIS. 35: (c) Joseph Sohm; ChromoSohm Inc/CORBIS; (tr) Robert Manella/Getty Images. 36: (bc) Gregory G. Dimijian/Photo Researchers, Inc. 36-37: (b) Creatas/PunchStock. 37: (b) Ken Karp for MMH. 38: John B. Boykin/CORBIS. 39: (br) ThinkStock/SuperStock; (t) Bill Pogue/Getty Images. 40: (br) Rosemary Calvert/Getty Images; (t) Lester Lefkowitz/CORBIS. 41: (br) Erich Hartmann/Magnum Photos; (tr) Jonathan Nourok/PhotoEdit. 42: (b) SEAFAIR Archive, Seattle WA; (tr) David Young-Wolff/PhotoEdit. 43: (c) Bill Pogue/Getty Images; (tr) David Young-Wolff/PhotoEdit. 44: (br) David Young-Wolff/PhotoEdit. 46: (tr) Ken Karp for MMH. R1: (br) George H. H. Huey Photography. R2: (cr) Dominique Braud/Animals Animals; (cr) LMR Group/Alamy Images; (tr) Tom Till/Tom Till Photography; (tr) John and Carol Rees. R3: (br) David Young-Wolff/PhotoEdit; (cr) Darrell Gulin/CORBIS; (cr) David Young-Wolff/PhotoEdit; (tr) AirPhoto USA/TerraServer.com; (tr) Garry Black/Masterfile. R4: (br) James Randklev /Getty Images; (tl) Charles McDowell/Grant Heilman Photography; (tr) Gary Buss/Getty Images.